Minimalism

Optimal Guidance For Organizing And Tidying Your Living Space: Efficient Strategies For Room-By-Room Decoration And Innovative Approaches For A Well-Structured Lifestyle

(Efficient Manual For Achieving Your Desired Lifestyle With Minimal Technological Dependence And Reduced Expenses)

Ismael Freire

TABLE OF CONTENT

Lead a Minimalist Lifestyle 1

Ways To Make Everything In Your Life Easier 13

QUANTITY OVER QUALITY PRIORITIZED Z 26

Zen and the Decluttering Technique 62

Living Rooms: Dining Room, Foyer, and Family Room 77

Sorting through your friend list 102

Enjoy Greater Independence 130

Lead a Minimalist Lifestyle

By now, you ought to know what minimalism is and how leading a minimalist lifestyle may benefit your life. We've also discussed how the fundamental idea of minimalism is to get rid of everything pointless and ineffective, particularly in the form of mental and physical clutter. Of course, clutter is a component of it, and we've spoken about a few strategies to deal with it, but clutter is just as much a result of a disorganized mind as it is a cause.

I want to share some ideas and tips in the following areas that I have found useful since starting to live a minimalist lifestyle.

Destroy outdated documents

Having a paper shredder at work makes it simple to get rid of paper clutter. So you should also purchase a personal paper shredder to keep your home office tidy and orderly. Anything that is no longer needed, such as outdated paperwork, should be destroyed.

Utilize a "basic" cell phone.

You may make it "basic," but don't worry, I'm not encouraging you to throw away your brand-new smartphone—though I might try to talk you out of buying one in the first place. I want you to take some time to consider which phone features or apps actually improve your life and which are just here to take up your space. Emails, social media, and many smartphones are available nowadays. These new models have some beneficial qualities but can also be distracting. Although they are incredibly helpful, smartphones also contribute significantly to stress. You may become disturbed and anxious by checking your social media accounts, reading your emails when you wake up, and reading about bad news stories. They might waste your time and energy as well. Consider disabling your notifications.

You should deactivate or disable your email and social media account notifications. They won't annoy you every time someone posts an update if you do this. To prevent unsolicited emails and other distractions, unsubscribe from anything that isn't necessary.

Activate your accounts on social media. You can think about deactivating your social media accounts if simply turning off your notifications isn't enough. Eventually, you'll conclude that Instagram, Twitter, and Facebook are insignificant. Even using social media, you should always remember that life happens offline. Being confident in your choices and free from the need to measure your life to others is a key component of minimalism. People tend to present the best versions of themselves, which are often fake. While comparing your life to others is common, doing so will ultimately divert you from your actual goals. Some suffer from FOMO. However, there are also many advantages to taking a sabbatical and gaining some perspective.

Social networking is a terrific tool for maintaining relationships with former acquaintances, but getting in touch with them is still preferable. Walls are wonderful, but nothing compares to a phone conversation, a postcard, or a face-to-face meeting.

Eliminate the majority of your credit cards.

Credit cards are great as a last defense against unfavorable financial circumstances. This money should only be utilized in an emergency, following the depletion of your savings and emergency fund. You should try your best to stay out of debt. Even worse, you should try to stay out of debt by not purchasing needless items. Although they could be helpful, credit cards can also be problematic.

Furthermore, having credit cards on you may encourage you to make unnecessary purchases. Therefore, it is best to carry cash rather than credit cards. Only carry the amount of money you need for the day. You'll have better control over your finances in this method.

Change up your daily commute.
Being a minimalist involves more than simply material possessions. It also involves making the most of your time and effort. Consider your daily commute in the morning. Do you believe you could travel more efficiently? It's not necessary to locate a faster path.
An easier approach can be found in its place. In this manner, you can enjoy your commute and make the most of the time by reading, meditating, or listening to music.

An alternative to driving or using the bus is to try walking. You can work out for twenty-five minutes in this manner. You can organize your thoughts and plan for the next day while you stroll.

Reduce speed

Inhale. Take your time. Because of how busy life may be, getting stuck in meetings, traffic, and many other things is possible. Enjoy some downtime and de-stressing. Savour the moment as it is. Engage in enjoyable activities. Consume your preferred cuisine.

Pay a visit to your loved ones. Take up new interests and make new acquaintances. Engage in meditation. Change things up. Leave your comfort zone behind. Remember that life is a finite resource, so make the most of it.

Make your to-do list shorter.
Live life fully, but avoid overcommitting to too many activities or duties. Although having objectives is good, you shouldn't have too many of them. To truly accomplish your goals, you have to be realistic.

In the same way, you should avoid working yourself to the point of exhaustion. Select the things that are essential for you to do and assign the rest to others. Postponing non-urgent duties is another option. Never be frightened to turn down an opportunity or anything you don't truly want to do.

Don't forget to pack a shopping bag.

Make sure you always bring your shopping bag when shopping. You may reduce the usage of paper and plastic bags in this way. This enables you to protect the environment and prevent further clutter.

Do not purchase supplies and storage boxes before completing the decluttering process.

Some become too enthusiastic to tidy up. They buy and stock a lot of containers because they expect to need a lot of them. But since it may leave you with more containers than you need, this is not a good practice. You wind up with more clutter instead of less.

Clear your head.

A busy schedule might cause mental congestion. Regular mindfulness meditation practice will help you clear your mind. Your ability to think clearly will allow you to be more creative, productive, and efficient. To meditate:

Look for a calm area.

Sit, shut your eyes, and concentrate on the here and now.

Steer clear of pointless thinking.

Return your attention to the here and now if you think like this.

Another option is to go on a thirty-day digital fast. Avoid using social media and internet browsing for pointless purposes. Use of your computer should be limited to very necessary situations. Reducing your digital use will improve your appreciation of offline existence. You'll have time to take in your surroundings, socialize, and develop new abilities.

Ways To Make Everything In Your Life Easier

Before we dive into this issue, we want to be clear up front that simple is challenging. You may devise a plan to simplify your problem, but you could find it hard to carry it through. It will still take work and some willpower to accomplish this. This chapter will concentrate on practical advice to help you begin the process of simplifying your life.

Simple Adjustments to Make Your Life Easier

Establish recurring objectives

Try to set one to three goals per month instead of all at the start of the year. This can assist you in forming new habits and breaking down more ambitious objectives into smaller, more achievable ones. You might be able to do tasks with this that you have been putting off for months or years.

Clear out your closet.

It's incredible how much refreshed you'll feel as you go about your day if your room and closet are tidy when you get up. Be honest: it's probably time to go with something if you haven't worn it in six months.

Employ a Pen and Paper

Although this is getting a little outdated, writing things down helps your memory recall them more easily. You can prioritize your duties by starting to write down the notes you take from emails and organizing your list in this manner. Moreover, writing down your responsibilities on paper will aid in concentration.

Simplify Your Morning Routines

Are you among the numerous individuals with such a hectic morning schedule that makes you want to just get out of bed and start your day? Make this part of the day easier by packing your clothes and lunch for the following workday the night before. Your morning routine frequently determines the course of your day, so if you can start the day relaxed and stress-free, you're more likely to stay that way than if you're up and down all morning.

Make sure you have a travel pack.

Make it a practice to keep an overnight bag prepared in your car in case you occasionally need to pack an unforeseen bag for work travels. Along with shampoo, conditioner, and clean clothes, keep some toothpaste in there.

Make use of a Crockpot.

Crockpots are low-cost and simple to operate. Simply toss in the food before leaving for work in the morning, and you'll have a ready-to-eat dinner when you get home! Doing this can reduce the time and cost of dining out. Do not let your lack of cooking experience frighten you. People who have never cooked before can use a crockpot with success.

Unsubscribe from this channel.

Sending irrelevant emails to yourself is a terrific way to squander time. Sort through your inbox and choose the email providers you don't want to receive anymore.

Put Your Bag in Order

Many people always carry rubbish and pointless objects in their backpacks or handbags. Examine yours to ensure that it is well-organized. Getting this resolved could affect your daily life more than you realize.

Make use of Google Drive.

Start storing your documents on Google Drive instead of carrying about your flash drive. This will help you avoid duplicate files and provide you access to them from anywhere. One of the best things you can do to simplify your life is to use Google Drive.

Arrange Your Workout

Without a strategy, before you begin your workout, you may find it difficult to motivate yourself to go to the gym or become worried and agitated, not knowing where to start. If you set aside dedicated time, you'll be better equipped to follow through on your workout goal. Establish measurable objectives to help you stay on course even when you don't feel like it.

Get Some Vinegar from Apple Cider

I know this seems like a weird suggestion, but you would be surprised at how many uses vinegar has. Remove wax and stains, unclog your sink, and even whiten your nails! This single product serves various purposes and may be used repeatedly.

Acquire Additional Audiobooks

Regarding saving time, podcasts and audiobooks can be invaluable resources. Why not learn something new every morning while making your commute to work? When traveling, reading fiction can also be a useful approach to accomplish two goals at once.

Adopt a One-tab Policy

I believe most of us who grew up with the internet have struggled with having too many open tabs. Shutting down a few tabs will greatly increase your productivity. Make it your mission to only have one open at a time, and you'll see a massive increase in productivity!

Create a Folder for Email Reminders

Make a folder for email follow-ups instead of letting your read emails pile up since you're unsure what to do after reading them. Pick a workday to review this, and make sure you respond to things on time.

Keep Healthy Snacks on Hand

Nowadays, most offices feature vending machines that tempt you with sweets and chips. However, giving in to these cravings won't benefit your body or mind in any way. To combat these urges, try to eat a nutritious diet and carry your snacks to work. Greek yogurt, coconut flakes, and mixed nuts are healthy snack alternatives. You can also bring hummus dip and chopped crispy vegetables. You will feel a lot better in no time if you replace your regular Coke with a couple of glasses of water.

Make Lists at Night

You should jot out your daily to-do list before bed instead of after you wake up. You'll unwind, sleep better, and wake up refreshed and ready to take on your objectives.

Go Slowly

Even in their leisure time, far too many individuals rush everything. If this describes you, it's time to take things slowly and more deliberately. This assists you in decluttering and streamlining your life. Plus, you won't make as many mistakes if you do things carefully and gently the first time.

Five Effective Habits to Remain Dynamic & Efficient

*You are not always able to handle everything.

You are not a robot; you are a human. Therefore, don't hold yourself to an unreasonable standard. Although there can be infinite alternatives, your resources might be constrained. Sort through the options and make thoughtful choices. Recognize that you can't do everything immediately and clear out the unnecessary stuff holding you back. It will be simpler for you to complete tasks at work without feeling pressured to take on more, even when you are positive that you can't handle everything, the more self-awareness you have. You must decide on your objective in advance.

It is useless to work without a clear aim in mind. Understand your goals and how you plan to reach them in sufficient time to enable you to be well-prepared. For example, you should identify the goals you have for your career long before you create a plan for its development or advancement. Encourage the practice of planning and having everything clear to prevent last-minute surprises.

Making use of the "NO" power

You are well aware of the impact of a resounding yes. Now that you know the importance of saying "no," how about making it a practice to say "no" to let go of unwanted and bad situations? It will be simpler for you to complete tasks without too many interruptions if you can get into the habit of saying "no" when appropriate. Saying "no" to what you don't want will make it easier for you to say "yes" to what you want. Gaining the ability to say no will help you concentrate on the tasks, allowing you to maximize productivity. Taking use of the inspiration

Make it a habit to strive for growth and development rather than settle for the status quo. You'll undoubtedly be successful in achieving your goals in life if you have that mindset. Test your level of motivation to achieve a particular objective regularly. You will undoubtedly find it simple to achieve your goals when you are continuously driven to act morally. * The less distracted you are by life's little pleasures, the more driven you are to get things done. Maximize the beauty of life Life is not about whining all the time. To see the vibrant pulse of life, look past the small things in life. Work honestly, savor the little things in life, and maintain integrity while at work. The mess will go away by itself.

QUANTITY OVER QUALITY PRIORITIZED Z

Often, the term "creative block" refers to a self-imposed limitation placed on the artist, leading her to strive for what she perceives to be the perfect work. The artist develops a habit of thinking that prevents her from producing poor-quality work. Regretfully, it implies that the creator is not producing anything. The rhythm that creative endeavors produce in a creator's mind and body is one of the traits of creativity. The creative process itself frequently emphasizes the rhythm.

For this reason, most artists counsel aspiring creators to focus more on output volume than quality. The artist is the one who creates quantity. Quality is an enigmatic quality that is hard to define and agree on.

The writers of THE CLASSIC BOOK "Art and Fear" suggest learning to accept failure. A creative's primary issue with quantity is the worry that most inventions won't succeed. Because of the potential social repercussions of failure, it is normal for creators to be terrified of them. According to "Art and Fear," most of your work should serve as a guide to help you reach the important production that will ultimately determine its quality. The book asserts that quantity comes before quality. For an artist to improve, they must continue to create. All of creation is based on the same premise. The majority of business mentors advise using the "Fail Fast" strategy. It implies that you should build several straightforward prototypes of the companies you would like to venture into and allow them to be introduced to the public. Those who are successful will bear the responsibility.

The following tactics are used by CREATORS, who can generate large quantities to continue producing.

CREATE A DAILY PROCEDURE:

A lot of successful writers set aside time each day to write. It also applies to artists and musicians. The most productive teams schedule regular time to meet and brainstorm features for the product, even in the field of software product development. Establishing a daily regimen for the process helps the body adapt to the rhythm of creation. Just as there are night creators, there are plenty of morning creators who work best in the wee hours of the morning. Having a regular schedule saves you from spending time "settling in."

SPECIFY A ROOM AND DETAIL ITS COMFORT:

Conflict must be avoided when you are engaged in the creative process. Having a dedicated space for the creative process is a strategy employed by several successful creators. They try to ensure that the area is cozy for sitting (or standing) and that the necessary supplies are easily accessible. Some even go so far as to customize the lighting and wall color to help induce a sense of flow in the mind. Teams of entrepreneurs have meeting spaces equipped with whiteboards, markers, presentation materials, and plenty of tea or coffee to keep everyone's minds and talks flowing.

TURN OFF YOUR CRITICAL MIND:

Using critical and logical reasoning, the critical brain—the metaphorical left brain—helps shield us from potentially harmful events. However, the critical brain most harms the creative process, especially when it comes to quantity-oriented creativity. The voice of the critical brain, which is always focused on what is wrong with your creation, will not stop speaking to you. Turn it off. You ought to be prepared to generate complete garbage in the generative, creative process. Just turn off your critical thinking; we'll see how to manage the quality issue in a later chapter.

NEVER HESITATE TO COPY:

You can begin with broad concepts and then develop a variation on those concepts by utilizing a specific feature of those concepts. Even though you might start with something familiar, you might be shocked to find yourself in completely foreign territory. Teams of entrepreneurs frequently employ this. They begin with familiar products and just change each feature until the product is what they know. If you create a container, you can start with a teacup and play around with its features until you develop some interesting pairings.

The myth of quality robs the creator of a crucial aspect of the creative life. The capacity to produce more and better works that might eventually materialize. The main muscle you develop, if you concentrate on quantity, is your creative ability. Using filters to narrow the permissible range makes moving from there to quality simple.

Section 6. A Simplified Approach to Clothing and Style

One element of your life that is sometimes neglected while trying to simplify is your wardrobe. Even if their closets are brimming with clothing, many people feel they have nothing to wear. As it happens, having too much clothing can make getting ready in the morning more difficult. You may make getting dressed daily easier and more fun by taking a minimalistic approach to your wardrobe and style.

What, then, does a minimalistic outfit look like? Simply put, it's made up of a few well-made, adaptable parts that you can mix and combine to create a wide range of looks. This entails letting go of fads that are only popular for a few months and concentrating on classic pieces that are always in style.

Purging your closet is a good place to start when designing a minimalist wardrobe. Take everything out of your closet and replace it with only what you regularly wear and adore. It's time to part with everything you haven't worn in six months to a year. This phase of downsizing your wardrobe can be challenging, particularly if you have sentimental links to certain pieces.

Prioritizing quality over quantity is another approach to streamlining your clothing. Lowering the quantity of clothing that ends up in landfills will save you money over time and lessen your environmental effects.

After you've reduced the number of items in your wardrobe and bought a few high-quality pieces, it's time to consider how to get the most out of each one. Making a capsule wardrobe is one method to achieve this. An assortment of clothes that can be combined and rearranged to create several looks is known as a capsule wardrobe. The secret is to select pieces that complement one another nicely so you can effortlessly assemble a range of looks without buying new clothing.

This will guarantee that everything you own functions properly. For instance, you may choose a neutral color scheme of beige, gray, white, and black. Next, a dress, a blazer, and some trousers. Lastly, add accessories like jewelry or scarves to give your clothing some individuality.

Making the most of your clothes can also be accomplished by dressing with awareness daily. Spend time considering what to wear and how it will make you feel, rather than just putting on whatever is clean out of the blue. Rather than just wearing what's trendy, choose clothes that make you feel good about yourself and confident.

You may simplify and enjoy dressing daily by putting quality before quantity and building a capsule wardrobe. Thus, set aside time to sort through your wardrobe, buy a few high-quality items, and dress mindfully every day. Your closet will appreciate the simplification.

Section Four

Streamlining Your Everyday Schedule: How to Set Priorities and Streamline Your Time

"Minimalism is not a sacrifice, it's a celebration of the things that matter most." - Joshua Becker, Jr.

One of the most important things about implementing minimalism in our daily lives is simplifying our routines. It entails learning how to streamline our time and set priorities so that we may concentrate on the things that matter. We may minimize stress, increase productivity, and maximize our time by streamlining our daily routine.

You can make your everyday schedule simpler.

Set priorities: Write down everything you need to do each day and rank them in order of significance.

Get rid of anything that isn't necessary for your everyday schedule.

Assign: Assign any work that another person can complete.

Automate: Any repetitious work that a machine can perform should be automated.

Streamline: Any task that can be completed more quickly should be streamlined.

Plan: Divide your day into manageable chunks of time and adhere to them.

To make it easier for you to implement simplicity into your life, I will go over each topic in detail with examples.

Set priorities:

Setting priorities is a crucial part of streamlining your everyday schedule. It entails compiling a list of the things you must complete each day and prioritizing them based on importance. This can assist you in making the most of your time and concentrating on what counts. The following advice can help you prioritize:

a) Create a List:

List all of your everyday obligations and chores, then rank them in order of importance.

One way to create a list of daily duties is to take a few minutes at the start of each day to jot down all the chores and obligations you must finish. These include personal objectives, errands, work tasks, and housework.

As an illustration:

Awaken at six in the morning.

Prepare breakfast.

Examine your emails.

Working on the A project

Get together with your teammates.

Make a dentist appointment.

Shop for groceries.

Get dinner ready.

Spend thirty minutes reading.

Set your alarm for 10:00 p.m.

You can create this list on a notepad, planner, or smartphone app, depending on what works best for you. After you've made your list, you can order items based on urgency and significance. This will enable you to maximize your time and concentrate on what counts.

b) Importance versus Urgency:

Ascertain the importance of each work and which ones are urgent. Important jobs are those that are necessary to achieve your long-term objectives, whereas urgent activities are those that must be completed right away.

One way to distinguish between important and urgent projects is to consider the repercussions of not finishing a task on time. Important jobs are those that are necessary to achieve your long-term objectives, whereas urgent activities are those that must be completed right away.

As an illustration:

A client's urgent email response is an urgent duty since it must be completed immediately and may impact your work.

Making a presentation for a meeting next week is a crucial chore if you want to achieve your long-term objective of impressing your supervisor.

You may prioritize your duties and maximize your time by determining which are important and urgent. This will enable you to maximize your time and concentrate on what counts.

b) Apply the Matrix of Eisenhower:

This matrix, which divides your chores into four categories—urgent and important, urgent but not important, urgent but not important, and not urgent or important—helps you prioritize your work.

Putting tasks into four categories—urgent and important, important but not urgent, urgent but not important, and not urgent or important—is one way to use the Eisenhower matrix to prioritize them.

As an illustration:

Taking a call from a sick family member who needs your assistance is both urgent and crucial.

Organizing a trip for the following year is important but not urgent.

Verifying notifications on social media is urgent but unimportant.

An hour spent scrolling through your Facebook feed is not essential or significant.

Using the Eisenhower matrix, you can maximize your time and prioritize your tasks. This will enable you to maximize your time and concentrate on what counts.

Incorporate the 80/20 Rule:

According to this rule, 20% of the work yields 80% of the results. Utilize this guideline to rank the twenty percent of your assignments yielding the most returns.

According to this rule, 20% of the work yields 80% of the results.

As an illustration:

20% of your work yields 80% of the results, such as meeting with a client to finalize a significant transaction.

Eighty percent of your work yields 20 percent of the desired outcome: responding to unrelated emails.

You may prioritize your chores and maximize your time by applying the 80/20 rule. This will enable you to maximize your time and concentrate on what counts.

e) Divide Up Large Tasks

Divide large jobs into smaller, more doable portions. They will become less overwhelming and more manageable as a result.

Dividing a major project that needs to be finished into smaller, more manageable jobs is an example of breaking big tasks into smaller, more manageable portions.

As an illustration:

Composing a research paper is a significant task.

Smaller, more doable portions:

Select a subject.

Investigate the subject.

Outline.

Compose the opening.

Compose the body.

Write the final paragraph.

Edit and proofread

Large projects can be less daunting and more manageable by being divided into smaller, more manageable pieces. This will enable you to maximize your time and concentrate on one task at a time.

Section Three

Getting Ready for the Jump

reducing and clearing off belongings.

Decluttering and downsizing fundamentally demand us to reevaluate and reinterpret our relationship with material stuff. I've learned to let go of material belongings since I travel a lot, but I recognize that not everyone feels the same way, particularly as we age. Whether it's an antique book or a small trinket, our possessions frequently hold memories and feelings attached to them. Giving these things can seem like giving up a part of our past. The fear of regret begins to set in as we become older. We often wonder, "What if I need this later?" even for items we haven't used in a long time. Additionally, there is the concept of "sunk cost," which refers to the need to hang onto things because of the time, money, and emotions we have spent on them. One common feeling associated with aging is losing control over one's youth, health, and independence. Our material belongings become a means of reversing this and providing stability in a world that is changing quickly. However, there is also the enormous amount of goods we gather throughout time. It can be easier to just ignore decluttering anything because the idea of doing so can be overwhelming. Physical difficulties also play a part. It's difficult to sort, lift, and organize things, especially if you have health or mobility concerns. And then there's this deeper, more poignant element: the reminder that we are mortal. Decluttering can be emotionally taxing since, particularly as one age, it might seem like preparing for death. Cultural and generational beliefs also influence our attachment to objects. War and economic hardship taught earlier generations to save and hang onto things. This stands in stark contrast to the more disposable world of today. When someone lives alone, belongings may unintentionally become friends, filling a void and making it more difficult to let go. Lastly, the sheer number of decisions that must be made while decluttering—keep, discard, donate, or sell—wears people out, especially those struggling with cognitive issues. It's a difficult, emotional trip that calls for tolerance and comprehension. Anyone helping older people declutter must have a thorough understanding of these nuances. The emotional terrain surrounding goods can be navigated with empathy, tolerance, and understanding. Decluttering ultimately involves making a place for fresh experiences, memories, and a feeling of lightness and freedom that can greatly enhance one's quality of life and generate physical space.

The packing guide for the minimalist.

My perspective on life and travel has changed due to adopting minimalism as a lifelong traveler. Shifting to a digital nomad lifestyle entails minimizing my material and mental burden by concentrating on the things that are necessary to support my profession and enhance my experiences. My go-to pieces of electronic equipment are a sturdy, lightweight laptop that is perfect for my job and a dependable charger. My smartphone serves as a lifeline, a communication tool, and a central location for entertainment in addition to being a gadget. I focus on transferring the maximum number of apps from the laptop to the smartphone. For many services, including banking, the phone app is more user-friendly. A secure VPN is necessary for internet access, and universal adapters are required for various regions. In coworking environments and traveling, noise-canceling headphones have become essential, and a portable charger ensures I'm always charged. I've mastered the art of the capsule wardrobe when it comes to clothes. It's about having adaptable pieces that are simple to combine and match, emphasizing quality and durability, particularly to fit different climates. The secret is to keep things simple and not overpack for every eventuality. It's easier to just buy what you need as you go. Keep a basic first aid kit and travel-sized quantities of your favorite items with you. Recall that little is more.

Keeping digital copies of important documents and a simple wallet that holds only cash, credit cards, and identification simplify managing paperwork and finances. An extra degree of security is added with an

RFID-blocking wallet. Simple travel needs include:

A collapsible water bottle for staying hydrated.

A reusable grocery bag for numerous uses.

A little travel cushion and eye mask for peaceful sleep.

Apps for productivity and banking help me stay digitally organized, and in non-English-speaking nations, language translation services are quite helpful. Then there are the random things like locks for my luggage, a multitool that is constantly inspected for airline compliance, and a notebook for recording ideas and recollections. I always have a little notepad with me in my pocket. However, I advise against packing a multitool unless you plan to check your bags. The most crucial item I carry is, above all, an adaptable mentality. A key component of traveling light is being willing to purchase and discard items as needed. Bringing what I use is more important than maybe needing something. This method makes my journey easier and fits well with a basic, ecological lifestyle. My goal in traveling is to see the globe without the weight of extraneous belongings. Intentionality is the essential idea. Each component in a pack needs to have a distinct role and purpose. A minimalist offers mobility, flexibility, and a seamless transition to the digital nomad lifestyle by concentrating on necessities and multipurpose things.

Budgeting, saving, and creating passive income sources are all part of financial planning.

It is crucial for anyone thinking about living a nomadic digital lifestyle to prepare financially. A minimalist strategy that emphasizes intentionality, clarity, and concentration in financial decisions can also be beneficial in this area. I've discovered that smart budgeting and creating passive income streams are crucial to maintaining my nomad lifestyle. Permit me to offer some learnings from my experience. The first step in creating a budget is carefully assessing your present spending. Be sure to evaluate your yearly and monthly expenses and how they vary before starting your digital nomad journey. Check the cost of living in the places you are considering visiting; resources like Nomad List are helpful.

Knowing how much it costs to live in different nations will help determine what kind of passive income you'll require. Making a budget for nomads is essential. Think about lodging, meals, coworking spaces, insurance, and transportation. Don't forget to budget for unforeseen costs. It's a dynamic process that needs to be reviewed and adjusted frequently. An emergency fund is essential when saving. Try to save up enough money to cover three to six months' worth of costs in case of unanticipated events like illness or periods of unemployment. Consider setting up a transition fund to pay for tech equipment, travel permits, and lodging. Examine your savings regularly to ensure they match your evolving spending and lifestyle. One excellent alternative is affiliate marketing, which allows you to earn commissions by recommending goods and services. Producing digital goods like e-books, online courses, and stock photographs can be profitable. If you're good at creating material, YouTube and blogging can be quite profitable, especially if they receive a lot of traffic. E-commerce strategies that eliminate the need for inventory maintenance, such as print-on-demand and dropshipping, are great. Living a minimalistic digital nomad lifestyle involves more than being frugal with your money, traveling light, and generating steady revenue streams to finance your journey. Being a frequent traveler means handling money, like traversing a constantly shifting terrain. Here's how I manage my finances while traveling the world. It is essential to diversify sources of income. Because the internet is an unpredictable place, it's dangerous to rely solely on one source. Employ internet technologies to streamline your life by automating payments, expenditure monitoring, and invoicing. Remember your tax requirements as well.

I mainly rely on digital banking regarding financial tools and resources, especially those that charge little or nothing for international transactions. YNAB and Mint, two programs that track expenses, have come in quite handy for me in keeping tabs on my expenditures. Apps for converting currencies are another essential tool for tracking spending in various currencies. Additionally, websites like Fiverr or Upwork might be great places to find extra money.

The minimalist approach is a financial concept rather than just a mode of transportation. Put needs above wants, but don't deprive yourself in the process; instead, emphasize usefulness and value.

Constant learning is yet another important factor.

It is the most important quality to be adaptable. Opportunities and financial requirements are ever-changing. Adapting your financial tactics to the shifting tides requires regular reviews and adjustments.

This meticulous attention to financial planning and management guarantees the viability and happiness of the digital nomad lifestyle. It's important to preserve mental tranquility and the ability to travel freely in addition to continuing to travel.

A purposeful, frugal financial strategy prepares the way for a fulfilling and long-lasting nomadic lifestyle.

Zen and the Decluttering Technique

Your crowded home will jar your senses and make you feel stressed. Your mind becomes preoccupied with thoughts like "Oh, I should finish this. I should put that away." because of all the clutter calling out to you. Furthermore, these objects' wide range of hues gently throws your head into disarray. Even in a messy home, the sensory overload can still be very subtly unpleasant.

The Objective and Role of Zen

Zen is a mental practice that facilitates single-minded attention. The mind gets liberated from the business of things by doing this. Tranquility and healing occur. Such an experience is best suited to a calm setting. A tidy home subtly fosters a mood that encourages emotions of contentment and tranquility. It is much simpler to deal with an onslaught of abrupt sounds in a quiet and peaceful environment. Naturally, it happens when your spouse or kids barge in the door after a long day at work. When you get home from work, it also works for you. Picture yourself falling into an easy chair when you get home from work. Imagine how relieved you will be to be free of the constant tapping of computer keyboards, the rustling that occurs as colleagues traverse the office floor, and the infrequent, animated talks. Take a seat and take in the silence for a bit.

Take a look at an online picture of a Zen garden. All left is one or two rocks that run parallel to curved lines in the sand. What makes it so seductive? Look at this beautiful image of desert dunes. Similarly, nothing exists there save the sun and the soft, rolling waves the wind raking across the sand creates. People adore those pictures. They evoke calming emotions that are captivating.

You must stop your mind's meanderings by the garden's scenery and the desert. You set aside those mental distractions briefly to marvel at the elegance of simplicity. Stress gradually gives way to serenity, and you start to feel at ease. You connect with the forces of your higher self, that priceless aspect of yourself that pulses and sways with life.

The Zen Method and Mindfulness

To manage his persistent pain, Dr. Jon Kabat-Zinn traveled to the East to study Zen meditation. He went through every phase of studying the Zen method. He introduced Mindfulness Meditation, a Westernized version, because it worked for him. Clinicians thoroughly investigated his procedures, with very successful results. Later, mindfulness practices were implemented in several fields.

To practice mindfulness, set aside some time to concentrate on the "here and now," either by paying attention to your breathing or a stunning scene (like the night sky). Mental discipline results from refusing to allow wandering thoughts, which have a cunning way of battering the conscious mind. This technique creates a calm and peaceful atmosphere.

For this reason, keeping your home tidy is crucial. It gives you mental room to concentrate without being sidetracked by clutter. Your belongings won't be lying around, tempting you to do other things. Rather than being driven by obligations, you are steadfast and anchored in your identity as a person.

The Skill of Decluttering and Its Advantages for the Brain

You've heard the labels "left-brained" and "right-brained." The "left brain" is linked to reason and conscious thought. Creativity and abstract thought are linked to the "right brain." The analogy is valid even though the two areas of your brain don't work independently. More tangible ideas like logical problem-solving, daily duties, and the distinct interpretation of events and experiences are handled by a specific region of your brain called the neocortex. It is a bustling location where information processing is necessary. Other parts of the "right brain" are responsible for things like coming up with original ideas, coming up with fresh approaches to problems that have come up recently, and expressing oneself creatively to let go of negative energy and interact with people without using words.

Your inventive, creative mind may work wonders when combined with your rational, practical thinking. Have you ever wondered how creative minds came up with original concepts and then applied those concepts to the logic of the computer industry? These guys create well-liked video games, graphics applications that create three-dimensional artwork from a two-dimensional screen, new useful software, etc. Similar to how music and art blend creativity, structure, and thought.

Microsoft and Apple are the products of a combination of practical knowledge and creativity. The best entrepreneurs succeed. They all do best in spaces that are free of clutter.

Chapter 3: How to Apply the KonMari Approach

We learned the fundamentals of the KonMari Method in the previous chapter. Allow us to examine how you might apply it in your daily life in this chapter. This is an outline of five points that you can use to start using the KonMari approach.

First Step: Get Rid of It! Throw away! Throw away!

Discarding items that don't matter to you is the first KonMari technique skill you should acquire. This encompasses everything, including mental and spiritual clutter, and is not limited to only tangible goods or material possessions. Before taking action, you should picture the life you believe will bring you happiness. You must go deeper for happiness than a well-organized sock drawer or closet. To genuinely be happy, you must purge your mind, body, and spirit. Everything that would bring you happiness should be a part of your perfect life. One of the main things that affects you and prevents you from having the time to pursue your aspirations is constantly having to deal with filth and clutter. Remember that getting rid of items you don't need will free up space for the things you value, desire, and love.

Step Two: Hold on to the Things You Love

"Spark of joy" is one of the main ideas of the KonMari method. In the culturally diverse nation of Japan, spirituality is deeply ingrained in daily existence. People think they can better enjoy life by being aware of their emotions. According to Kondo, everything that does not "spark joy" for you should be thrown away. Remove everything you own from a category and use your senses to feel, touch, and experience it. Take it over in your hands and give it a close examination. Attempt to comprehend your feelings over it. If you were to throw it away forever, how would you feel?

Since "spark joy" is subjective, it could not always be logical. Try to follow your intuition rather than second-guess the logic of your preferences. For example, save something that makes you happy despite being useless but has a special place in your heart. Anything that gives you second thoughts might not be worth preserving, but if you are determined to keep it, don't listen to what others say.

Step 3: The Prison of Procrastination

We constantly lie to ourselves, which may surprise you. These could be tiny white lies or enormous white lies. We all have excess clothes, books, craft supplies, and other items we hold onto, thinking we might need them in the future. Recall that something does not necessarily have to be something you enjoy or that you will need it in the future.

Try to picture all the stored items carefully to utilize them in the future.

Clothes, magazine clippings, cables, cosmetics, and other items might be among them. Now, consider the rationale behind your attachment to them. You'll notice that most of these things have been stored safely because you're worried about them or don't want them to go to waste. Most of these are just lame justifications like "What if I need it later?" It's admirable that you can plan and remain organized, but if these things take up unnecessary space in your life, you should eliminate them. It is best to discard these items if they are causing you issues in your life.

Personification is the fourth step.

You must regard things as though they are sentient beings with feelings. When you get home, would you ever hang a friend in a dirty corner or dump a cat on the bed? Similarly, never discard clothing or other objects; instead, store them carefully in their proper locations. Try to keep your drawers organized rather than cramming them with random items. Things will get disorganized as soon as you start losing track of them. To determine what to keep and discard, Kondo suggests gathering all your stuff in one category—clothes, for example—and arranging them all at once. This can help you determine how many items you own and how many are worthless junk. She thinks keeping things in plain sight will keep your belongings organized and mess-free. Never distribute items carelessly or toss them around.

Step Four: You Are Reflected in Your Closet

According to Kondo, your closet reflects your thoughts, which explains why you find it hard to part with some items. According to Kondo, you should refrain from throwing away or giving away some things because you want to keep them for a longer period or sentimental reasons.

She claims that you are scared of feeling bad about discarding some things. You will quickly discover that your desk drawer has dozens of items you haven't even remembered owning or seeing in years.

Things like these are pointless and ought to be thrown away. Most of these might evoke recollections from the past, both good and bad, but they are still only memories. According to Kondo and her method, all that matters is the now, and anything that prevents you from enjoying it should be thrown away. Even though these antiques may have sentimental value for you, they are a nuisance in your daily life and have no place in the present. This implies that you must eliminate them to free up space for your present.

Living Rooms: Dining Room, Foyer, and Family Room

The best place to start when decluttering your home and simplifying your lifestyle is in the living spaces, where most "stuff" tends to congregate. Since most people spend most of their time in these spaces at home, many objects that can become overwhelming find their final resting place there.

All of the unnecessary goods in these rooms won't need to be thrown away or donated; instead, you should consider whether they truly need to be there now. Even if a place isn't quite minimalist yet, sometimes simple rearrangements can make it more logical, stylish, and functional.

Eliminating the Superfluous

Eliminating unnecessary items from these locations is the first step towards organizing and decluttering this space. Look through your old toys, periodicals, novels, and décor for your family area. You may have intended to create a collage using the 2009 magazine as inspiration, but you won't get there soon. Examine any remaining toys to determine whether any are damaged or lacking parts. If so, either discard them or donate them. In this area, décor is very important. If something takes more than five seconds to dust and has no sentimental value, it is usually unnecessary. Check-in your dining room in the same manner. If the dining room table isn't used frequently, it becomes another place where we leave items lying around and never clean them up again. Your liquor cupboard is another prominent location in the dining area; purge the items you will never use.

The foyer is the last location where you can discard unnecessary items. This will include accessories, coats, and shoes that either won't fit or that your partner and kids will never wear again. Since the foyer is the first area you see when you enter your house, it is essential to a minimalist lifestyle. It should be as straightforward as possible.

Show your kids the piles you wish to donate or discard, and then let them take whatever they want to return to their bedrooms. (We'll arrive there in no time.)

Easygoing

These sections' general layout and lines should be kept uncomplicated and tidy. Refrain from going overboard with decorations, whether wall hangings or tangible items. If you purchase brand-new furniture, try to purchase basic items as well. Suppose your television can be mounted on the wall. In that case, there's no need to purchase an extravagant entertainment center because the extra room will only encourage "stuff" to find its way into the drawers and onto the shelves. A sleek, all-in-one sofa will be far easier to maintain than a sofa with eight cushions you must change around daily, so choose simple, level furniture.

To make these spaces feel cozy, add some décor, but keep it basic and uncomplicated: a picture frame, a coffee table book, or a vase filled with flowers.

Concentrate

The storage for items you will be doing regularly should be your main focus in these areas. It can be difficult for a family that is so accustomed to television to give it up, even if some minimalist families do. You will need to keep DVDs and Blu-rays if your family watches them. Invest in a case that can carry all the disks rather than 250 plastic boxes. You can discard the boxes and store the case more easily. Use cabinets or boxes to keep everything out of sight. Cutlery and china should be stored in cupboards or drawers in the dining room rather than being left out on the table, as this isn't hygienic.

You will need some storage for the entrance. You might wish to spend some money on basic hooks if you don't have a front-hall closet. The person can only have as many belongings as that one hook can hold, and you should only retain as many hooks as your family members. You can also use a basket or box to store items like dog toys, shoes, or umbrellas. You shouldn't have too much in your foyer other than that. Any other items a youngster may have are best off staying in their room.

Cut off

Remaining disconnected from technology entails having less of it around than usual. Is a phone always within 10 feet of you really necessary? You should have a house phone in a central location if you still use one, which you should because it is safer. The same holds for a TV. Keep the TV in the family room if you can't break the habit or want one in case something unexpected happens. Watching TV in the dining room or kitchen only ruins meaningful family time. Phone and laptop cords are another major cause of clutter; get rid of them. Try giving phones a time limit and then hiding them for extended periods. This will eliminate trip risks from your living areas and protect your phone from normal wear and tear.

It's important to consider illumination as well. One overhead light will make things easier and simpler than four or five table lamps. Although those individual lights may seem cozy and straight out of a magazine, how much longer will it take them to light up or clean? Purchase powerful LED lights, and you'll be done with it all.

Starting Now: Get Rid of All the Distractions in Your Life

Simplifying your life is the first step towards adopting a minimalist lifestyle. To do this, you must reduce the distractions and clutter that have been consuming your time and energy, both inside and externally. This chapter shows you how to get rid of everything holding you back and keeping you from living life to the fullest. You are already a minimalist just by deciding to clear out this extra stuff.

The method you choose to eliminate this mess is really up to you. Most people have found that there are no hard and fast rules. No minimalism criteria or guidelines say you can't call yourself a minimalist unless you've given away 1,000 things to charity. Starting your Journey to minimalism is easier when you acknowledge that you are already one. To become a minimalist, you must follow your response when making decisions by asking yourself, "What would a minimalist do?"

Everybody experiences decluttering differently. Some find it challenging to part with the first few things, but with time, it gets easier. On the other hand, other people feel the opposite, and as time goes on, they begin to justify holding onto things. Breaking those links can be difficult, but that's why it's a journey.

The elimination of waste is at the center of the minimalist lifestyle philosophy. When it comes to waste, anything unnecessary is viewed as a luxury. But the beauty of minimalism is that it's always associated with being green, inexpensive, and living in harmony with nature.

*Clutter-free living

*Getting rid of harmful people in your life, clearing out

Here are a few ideas to help you declutter your life.

Outfits

Ensure that the open side of every hanger for clothing in your closet faces outside the closet. Afterward, return anything you wear to its original state and remove anything left out of your closet. For a few weeks, store these leftover clothing somewhere safe. It is probably preferable to break up with them if you won't be using them for this amount of time. Apply the same method to the clothes that aren't put up to eliminate the items you haven't worn.

Electronics and technology

All your outdated computers, mobile phones, music players, and cameras you are not using should be recycled. The books and DVDs you always say you'll look at again but are not going to are either sold or given away.

Eliminating poisonous people from your life

Numerous terms have been used to describe easily losing oneself in one's job, such as concentration, focus, flow, and escapist. It can be identified when you can tune your brain to focus on a particular task and blur the background around you. Put another way, it's your sweet spot—a period when you perform well. The surrounding world vanishes as your whole cognitive effort is concentrated on that one task at that precise instant.

Everyone finds it difficult to stay focused at some point in their daily lives. When there are too many distractions, your brain cannot focus on any task, such as completing assignments at work or projects around the house. For this reason, it's a good idea to teach yourself how to focus and lose yourself in your task. To accomplish this, you must comprehend the true processes in your brain when you develop this mindset.

There are various causes for being sidetracked. Fear of failing, moving on, achieving, or finishing could be one of the causes. Boredom or a lack of enjoyment from your work could be another factor. On the other hand, you might be resisting. A negative force called resistance prevents you from doing any action promoting long-term development, integrity, or health but instead resists instant enjoyment. This keeps you from ascending to a higher nature in the end. You could also become sidetracked if you believe you cannot complete the assignment. Perhaps you tell yourself that you are unworthy, unprepared, or not as good as others. Lastly, you might be diverted just because you are acting incorrectly.

Most of the time, we create our internal congestion. Most people will check Facebook, Twitter, email, and other social media hundreds of times on a dull day. The majority of the time, there is nothing to check in the first place. We appear to indulge ourselves with easily accessible distractions without reluctance, whether the source is our minds or our pockets. Lastly, internal clutter can be brought on by stress.

You miss out on special moments when you are preoccupied with updates on your ex-classmates children on your social media feed. For example, Joshua Bell, one of the most well-known classical musicians of all time, performed 45 minutes of Bach on a 3.5

million dollar violin in a Washington, DC metro subway station, earning only thirty-two dollars. Most people were so preoccupied with their hectic schedules that they hardly saw him playing one of the greatest pieces of music ever recorded.

The good news is that you can manage your internal distractions using a variety of solutions. Let the answering machine handle your calls and take your phone off the hook. When you have something to do on your computer, turn off the email notifications. Keep yourself to yourself in your workspace and keep out of the refrigerator, company, and entertainment gadgets. Finally, deal with any possible distractions as quickly and discretely as possible. For instance, if you come across a simple work you can finish quickly, do it; otherwise, put it on your to-do list and return to it later if there are more important things to attend to.

Additionally, you should develop the ability to move forward despite any anxieties that might deter you. Remind yourself that you are not perfect and that errors will always occur. But what the heck? Since no one is flawless, accept responsibility for your errors and go on. If your mind is being overtaken by boredom, reward yourself when you finish the activity or take a quick break to engage in something enjoyable.

You can overcome the resistance that leads to diversions by behaving professionally. Being professional entails putting in the required time and being there every day. However, if emotions of inadequacy are taking over, just keep in mind that you are always doing your best and that there is nothing more you can do. Additionally, skill-training programs and confidence-boosting chances are available. Take a break if you have the time. Let your subconscious finish the assignment while you sleep on it.

The best strategy to deal with distractions caused by stress is to try to find the humorous side of situations that could otherwise make you anxious.

Everyone has to deal with things like flat tires, failing to see an exit on a highway, making poor decisions that have consequences, and lengthy lineups. Don't let your attention become so consumed by what transpires that you fail to see the humor in these situations. Discovering its opposite is all that's required in life.

Examine Your Spending Patterns and Project Future Costs

Knowing where your money goes is one of the most important things to include in a minimalist budget. List all your money over the last few months and classify your purchases and outlays.

When using a credit card, your purchases are frequently automatically categorized by your credit card statement; otherwise, you can use the following list to help you keep track of your expenses.

Some of your costs will be fixed, meaning they won't fluctuate monthly. A few instances of fixed costs are:

- Tenant
- Mortgage
- Auto financing
- Payment of insurance premiums

Other costs are variable, meaning they could change from month to month based on outside variables or decisions you make:

- Utilities (which can change depending on how much you use them and the weather)
- Subscriptions for cable, phone, internet, and other services
- Food
- Transport
- Clothing and personal hygiene
- Health care costs
- Amusement
- Journey
- Presents
- Additional categories (kids' activities, pets, hobbies, fitness, etc.) that you may find relevant

Perform a quality check once your expenses have been listed and arranged. Do the costs and contributions to your savings from the previous month truly equal your income? It's simple to keep track of all your expenses (or at least the locations where you spend the money) if you pay with a credit or debit card. If you withdraw from an ATM or bank, you must diligently document your cash withdrawals and how the money was spent.

Many of the expenses you find when you review your budget should be no surprise; if you have a mortgage, this is the amount you agreed to pay. Most of your monthly costs for transportation, groceries, and service subscriptions will likely remain consistent.

But watch for spending levels and categories that catch you off guard. For example, did you realize how much you spent each month on new clothes or dining out? Does this amount of expenditure align with your priorities and long-term objectives? A minimalist budget must be created and adhered to, which requires you to become conscious of your financial behavior and balance it against your true financial goals.

You must now project your future spending in each category. Since this is the same amount you have previously spent, estimating your fixed expenses is simple. Use the updated amount if you expect a change (for instance, if you know your rent will go up the next month).

It will require some judgment and decision-making to estimate variable expenses. When expenses fluctuate erratically or because of unforeseeable circumstances, you can compute the average monthly expenditure for every category to make plans. Calculating an average is simple: just sum up all of the monthly expenses you monitored in the past, then divide the total by the number of months. For instance, if your grocery expenditures for the previous three months were $400, $600, and $500, your monthly average would be ($400 + $600 + $500) / 3 = $500.

Some variable costs could change predictably. For instance, if you live in an area where summers are extremely hot, you might use the air conditioner more throughout the summer, which would increase your power bill. By looking at your past spending patterns and extrapolating them into the future, you may estimate the predictable variations in your expenses.

After finishing your expense analysis, You should have a list of expense categories and an expected expenditure amount for each category. The following section will show you how to use this information to create a budget. Create a budget for the upcoming month to determine how much to set aside for variable expenses. Once you've mastered this, you may carry out the same procedure for months, when your variable expenses might vary. You will discover later in the chapter how to update your budget by reviewing and maintaining it and how to include expenses that don't occur regularly.

Sorting through your friend list

Life is indeed somewhat similar to Facebook. You make pals during your life. You might consider a few of these to be close pals. Some will only be acquaintances, while yet others will have a detrimental impact on your life. People's self-perception is influenced by their willingness to be used by others, which is one of the reasons they lack motivation to be productive. Eliminating items is only one aspect of minimalism. It has to do with eliminating unfavorable influences from your life.

Sort your pals into those who make you feel good about who you are and those who take away from your life. To some extent, you might be partially to blame. People who lack confidence frequently allow others to take advantage of them because they believe it validates them. It has the opposite effect. It gives you the impression that you are worthless unless you are helping or valued by others.

This is not a nice way to be at work. You might be one of those needy people who seem to crave validation more than others. Do you look to others for approval before taking any action? Do you put forth effort to impress? Do you make an effort to work harder than other people? Do you let many negative thoughts about your job linger in your head? You are your greatest enemy, so if you can answer "yes" to any of these, you should change how you live. Put yourself first, and stop attempting to please other people. By doing that, you avoid wasting time seeking approval from others.

Instead of constantly worrying about what other people think, you can give your workload priority. Additionally, you can schedule breaks and all the activities that help you gradually increase your stamina during the day.

Examine your buddy list to determine which of your pals drain your time and energy, and consider if it's your responsibility or theirs. It's worthwhile to hang onto a relationship if it requires reciprocity. If everything is given, it's time to let go and quit attempting to win over folks who don't have the time. Your life becomes much simpler and less complicated, and you have more time to be productive.

Feeling appreciative

There will be less in your possession, but you will be more appreciative. When you focus just on the important aspects of life, you'll quickly realize that countless habits no longer rule your existence. You maintain a comprehensive perspective on your life and can intentionally enjoy moments by perceiving them more mindfully. You'll have a greater capacity for gratitude. Feeling thankful for what you have as well as for everything you lack. Thankful for the people in your life that truly matter a lot. Thankful for life's wonderful moments, health, and happiness. Thankful for life.

comfort

The simple lifestyle will help you when you move and travel as well. You will feel uneasy that you have forgotten something as you let go and realize you are unsure what to pack. The minimalist lifestyle makes these decisions a lot simpler. You also have an easier time responding to the following questions because you have fewer items:

What must I bring with me?

How should I store it?

How many bags are necessary for me?

You realize that living a minimalist lifestyle implies having fewer possessions, which reduces stress.

time savings

In life, material possessions and consumer items are secondary. But the most crucial aspect of existence is time. You'll discover that leading a minimalist lifestyle will give you more time on autopilot. You will have a lot more time because fewer items will be inspected, fixed, and cleaned. Being a minimalist will always save you time, somehow. That's because things are more organized and tidy. It frequently happens that the wardrobe is unduly cluttered, especially with ladies. You should consider organizing your closet as a lady. You won't regret it, I'm sure, once you make your decision. You'll find the perfect dress much more quickly. For instance, when garments that are truly too big, too small, too bold, or associated with a particular memory fall out of the closet, you start to consider things more carefully. Ultimately, you gain new skills in addition to saving time. There are important things you can do with this extra time.

well-being

It is better to eat less but healthier, should be the catchphrase. Most of the time, adopting a minimalist lifestyle can also lead to a healthier one. Time, space, and energy have already been spared. One is inherently happier and has more time for life's meaningful pursuits. Naturally, one's health benefits from this. You eat healthier in the end, there is less stress, and everything is more controlled. Naturally, adopting a minimalist approach to nutrition and allocating the funds toward purchasing Fairtrade or organic items would be beneficial. Better eating less, but healthier, ought to be the catchphrase.

inventiveness

Do creativity and minimalism go hand in hand?

Of course, some people manage their fast-paced lifestyles and consumerism sensibly without leading minimalist lives and are nonetheless creative. Living a minimalistic lifestyle is not a prerequisite for being creative. However, there are two stages to the creative process.

1. examination

You must first confront the difficulty or issue and analyze it. To address the problem, you're searching for motivation and inspiration.

Second incubation

The subconscious handles the issues while consciousness takes a break. One important idea that helps solve the situation is mentioned. Living a minimalist lifestyle might encourage creativity because one intentionally creates a "lack" that is ultimately not viewed as a lack. Cutting oneself apart from many things helps one focus on what matters. Consider the following query, for instance:

"How would I feel better?"

You must come up with a unique response to that query. Finding solutions is almost forced when we approach an issue or task puristically.

Of course, minimalism has many other benefits, but those may vary depending on how you apply and live the philosophy. Can your mood and quality of sleep get better? You will naturally become weary early and fall asleep more soundly and quickly if you avoid driving. The immune system also becomes more stable when one spends time outside. You notice that your skin is more beautiful due to paying attention to your diet, which ultimately improves your focus. One's life will become more aware, and a vacation may not lead to the final location on Earth but fully into the environment. It is astounding how few people genuinely understand their own country. You become more at ease, and since you might not own the newest smartphone, you don't always need to use it for communication, which enhances social contact. Thus, a minimalist lifestyle opens up new avenues and offers you many benefits. The minimalist way of living impacts every aspect of life. This is something to remember as you carefully consider your minimalist lifestyle.

Chapter 4: A Tiny House Lifestyle

Are you prepared to take it further and switch to a basic living environment now that you incorporate minimalism into every aspect of your life? Recently, tiny homes have gained popularity as a kind of trend.

A growing number of people worldwide are adopting compact homes. You may think it's a terrible idea and wonder why anyone would want to go from a big, roomy house to a little, claustrophobic one.

It all depends on how you frame it, though. It's not a requirement for living a simple lifestyle or a way to set yourself apart from others. If all you need to survive is the bare necessities, you might want to get a little house.

Moving into a smaller location has several advantages, which I will outline for you so you can see how it will help you. In the end, it's always your decision.

You do not have to try everything other minimalists do just because you identify as a minimalist. You'll discover that most city authorities dislike tiny home builders.

This is because they all rely on the revenue from the construction of big houses. Energy firms will suffer a loss if individuals begin constructing their own solar-powered homes.

Since small homes are more self-sufficient, businesses that offer services to large households would lose business. When you resist paying the extravagant fees that construction companies, loan sharks, and banks demand for your substantial house investments, they lose out.

You wouldn't have to adhere to many societal norms that nowadays only add stress to our lives if you choose to live in a tiny house. Living smaller has more advantages than you can probably imagine at this point.

Advantages Of Relocating to a Tiny House:

The most obvious advantage of living in a little house is that, when compared to a large house, you will save a ton of money. A smaller house will only set you back a small portion of what an enormous apartment or mansion might. This is true whether the house is newly constructed or already built. If you have a smaller place, you can always save money on everything—maintenance included. You are undoubtedly aware of how expensive apartments are nowadays if you rent one. Invest in a tiny house rather than wasting money on a place that is not yours. For those who cannot afford to buy a property, renting is a short-term option, but in the end, it's just your money going into someone else's account in exchange for using their place. Instead of waiting years to collect enough money for a huge house, saving up for a modest one is much easier, and the relocation will happen sooner.

Many people are drawn to them because compact homes are so much more environmentally friendly. Compared to large homes, tiny homes consume a lot less resources. Most tiny home communities are extremely aware of their carbon effect on the environment and rely on solar power for electricity. To begin with, a little house takes up less room, making more room for extra occupants and animals. Living in a tiny house can lead to a very fulfilling existence. In addition to producing more electricity than they consume, residents in tiny home communities frequently cultivate their food and coexist peacefully. Vehicles can also be shared by many people in the spirit of simplicity, as opposed to everyone having one and increasing costs and emissions.

You'll also save a ton of time with a tiny home. It takes a lot of time to clean, mend, maintain a large house, etc. A fraction of that time will be needed for a tiny residence. You may spend time doing something productive or soothing instead of squandering it on pointless chores.

You are forced to get rid of a lot of stuff in your life when you move into a small area. When moving into a little house, you must let go of much worldly stuff. If you choose to move with items, it could be a significant source of tension. You must bring them with you and make room for them in your new residence. Why not start over and leave them behind? Having materialistic belongings is one burden you can simply let go of.

Building a tiny home allows you to surround yourself with more green space. Living in a minimalist compact house with a big garden is something you will undoubtedly adore if you are a nature lover. It allows you to plant trees or flowers, cultivate food, and offer your dogs extra room to play. For pets who have spent most of their lives caged up inside large houses, it may be a liberating experience, and it can be as liberating for you.

Many people have recently started purchasing mobile homes rather than simply purchasing a little house on land. This gives people who enjoy traveling a great deal of freedom. Committing to a place you might grow tired of or simply detest in the future is unnecessary. Living in a little house on wheels may be a lot of fun. Most locations provide sections where mobile homes are free to dwell for as long as they like. If you want to go above and above, give it a shot. These mobile homes are a very practical solution for people who work from home and typically only require their computers. When traveling, you can work from any place and take full advantage of the experience.

Constructing a little house can be a really special opportunity. Although you may always purchase one that has already been built, creating one allows you to add your unique style. You are free to customize it to your preferences and needs. You don't need to spend much money hiring a large crew of construction workers and expensive machinery. The folks who currently occupy them built many of the tiny dwellings. Although you can always add more staff, consider the savings in costs. Take advantage of this chance to express yourself creatively via your house. The outcome will take you by surprise in a good way.

Tiny homes in the nation are typically exempt from building code laws. This eliminates the inconvenience of dealing with officials that restrict your options. It offers you total autonomy and control over the style of home you desire. This also holds for your minimalist lifestyle. You shouldn't allow others to tell you what to do or not do. Stay loyal to who you are.

Decorating a tiny house doesn't need a lot of work or money. All it takes is a few things to bring some coziness and individuality into the room. Your savings are substantial, allowing you to purchase items that truly appeal to you. You shouldn't worry about filling up excessively large homes with many ornamental items, paintings, and vases. Living simply is far wiser.

Tiny dwellings spare you from the hassles and endless worry of dealing with mortgage troubles or con artists. Why settle for a massive new home that won't let you enjoy it because it will only cause more troubles in your life?

An additional benefit is that building a tiny home is significantly faster than building a large apartment or suburban house. You may construct the ideal little house for yourself in a few months.

Most of your spending will be reduced if you live in a compact home. You can use the money you save for things that are more meaningful to you. This might be used for your kids' schooling, loan repayment, emergency savings, and even more to treat yourself to a trip or activity you enjoy.

Reducing your living expenses also releases pressure to work more and make more money. You can get by if you live in a tiny home and have a regular wage. This eliminates the desire to compete with your peers and reduces stress. When you live in a large home and have bills to pay all the time, this can be a very big load.

You become closer to the people you live within a small environment. Huge homes with distinct rooms can impede communication and cause a sense of separation. When given freedom, people tend to lose themselves in their selves. Take advantage of the chance to live close by to strengthen your bond. You'll see you have much more time to truly enjoy each other and spend with your loved ones.

Most people start putting things they aren't utilizing in their guest room or a similar room. These are frequently things we never use but don't want to get rid of. They might contain hopes for the future or recollections of the past. It's possible that you used something once or twice before putting it in the guest room, sincerely thinking you would use it again later, but you never did. Now is the moment to remove these things from your closet or guest room and move them out of your life.

To ensure you have enough time to fully complete the activity, you should dedicate a few hours. Ensure you finish everything in a single day and don't put anything off. When organizing, we frequently tell ourselves that we will work on it more later. Then, we just close the door and "forget" to complete the task. That is not what you want to do in this room. If we are not careful, this is one of the most hazardous rooms in our houses. Therefore, you better finish it all in a single day. You may want to take breaks throughout the procedure, but don't give up until the job is finished.

To finish this challenge, begin in one of the room's corners. Attempting to complete everything at once is not necessary. One task at a time can be your concentration, and you can take your time. One package at a time, first, then another. Take your time moving through the space. Set aside specific spaces for trash, goods for donations, things you wish to sell, and things you want to keep. After you've gone through everything, you can return the objects you wish to keep to their appropriate storage places. That day, the remainder ought to be handled. Toss out anything you don't need, load up the car with the donation bin to drive it to the donation drop-off location, and list anything you wish to sell. Set a deadline for the things you are selling. If they still haven't sold after seven days, put them in the donation bin and keep adding one item per day for the rest of the challenge.

Take some time to freshen up your guest room after cleaning it out. Vacuum, wash the windows, open the blinds, and flip the bed. Give the space some vitality to rescue it from the mausoleum of materialism it once belonged to. Once you've finished, write in your daily notebook about how it felt to address these things and come to terms with who you were, who you are, and who you truly want to become.

Day Five

"You make a mistake when you say, 'If I had a little more, I should be very satisfied.'" You wouldn't be happy if your possessions were multiplied if you weren't happy with what you had.

- Charles Spurgeon

We frequently keep items in our dressers that we no longer need or want. You will give some of the things you no longer need to a charity or organization so they can be distributed to others in need today. This ought to be a rather easy task. Using a plastic shopping bag, head into your wardrobe and fill it with things you no longer need or want. Give the products to those who truly need them, and rejoice that your wardrobe is now considerably lighter and much easier to keep organized with fewer pieces.

It can feel nice to eliminate items you don't wear anymore. It assists you in recognizing your true self and your false self. We become honest with ourselves about who we are when we hang onto things we no longer fit into or don't wear. Frequently, we cling to these objects mainly because they serve as symbols of who we believe we are or would like to be, enabling us to wish in private that we were someone else. This has several detrimental side effects, some of which may harm one's confidence and sense of self. The best action is to eliminate these items while keeping the clothes you regularly wear and enjoy.

You can also dispose of any clothing that is torn, overly worn, or stained while you're at it. Keeping these things around to satisfy your physical attachment to your memories is not good for your health because they are no longer functional.

After going through your whole wardrobe and packing your bag for donations, place the things in your larger donation bin so you can get them to the donation drop-off when the challenge is over. Place your daily item in the box as well. You can then start your daily journal. With this, day five of your 30-day challenge will be over.

You can live a minimalist lifestyle daily.

It takes time to become minimalist and doesn't end one day. It's a way of thinking and life you embrace and practice daily.

To better comprehend this principle, let's revisit the preceding parallels. You don't give up on it even after you reach your target weight. You must keep it going. Even though you might experience obstacles along the path and occasionally consume highly processed food, you don't revert to your previous behaviors. You have to carry on with your healthy lifestyle.

When you decide to manage your money carefully, you don't give up easily, even if you achieve your objective—becoming a millionaire. You must keep it going. You can lose your millions and get into debt once more if you return to your previous habits.

When you have children, your role as a parent doesn't end when they graduate, get married, and start their own family. Depending on your children's life stage, your job as a parent may change, but you will always be their parent—day in and day out, year after year.

Similarly, after you decide to practice minimalism and concentrate on what matters most, you make the daily decision to follow through on this aim until it comes naturally to you.

It might be thought of as a habit that you grow into. Minimalists continue to choose minimalism; their decisions naturally become more sensible with time. They don't suddenly decide to quit being a minimalist and announce themselves as the best. They continue to act and put in the effort. They choose minimalism and live it every day.

Are you prepared to make the initial move?

Enjoy Greater Independence

Material belongings belong to you, not the other way around. But the latter is more likely to occur when you're overly dependent on material possessions.

Toddlers are probably your least favorite guests if you have a priceless collection on display in your house, are they not? What would happen if someone attempted to grab a piece or ran into the display? You try to stop others from bringing kids over because the possibilities above are upsetting. Such limitations could put needless distance between you and family members with young children.

You may worry before and throughout your travels because of your belongings. Of course, you don't want priceless items to be taken. You don't want your home's components and belongings to sustain additional damage. Living with an untrustworthy person exacerbates your concerns. Ultimately, you return home earlier than anticipated or choose to remain at home. If you pack expensive items like jewelry, thinking they will be safer with you, you can find yourself constantly striving to keep them safe while traveling. That will only make for a boring trip.

You will be more welcoming to any loved ones who may like to visit you if you are free from that excessive attachment to worldly possessions. Also, when you travel, you have fewer worries. Additionally, minimalism releases you from thoughtless consumption, tedious cleaning, and pessimistic thinking.

Give Priorities Your Whole Resources

Saving energy, money, and time is not minimalism's main goal. Instead, the way of living is how you allocate the necessary resources to what you deem important.

The best way to define priorities is as the things that take up most of your resources. However, there are situations when the things you list as priorities don't demand the most of your time and energy. You can't claim, for example, that your job comes first if you spend all of your free time traveling and having fun. If you can't even find a moment to speak with your parents, husband, or child, you can't claim it's your family.

The distractions in your environment can contribute to your perplexity. For example, some people mistake cleaning for an indication of productivity. In any case, it's preferable to ignore the mess. The best scenario, though, is when you don't have a lot of cleaning to do so you can concentrate more on your main work.

Purchasing a large number of discounted goods during sales is another example. It seems like a significant financial savings.

The best strategy to save money during sales is to avoid unforeseen costs. This is something to keep in mind if you consider financial security to be important.

If you're a parent, your youngster may not comprehend why you put in so much effort even if you buy them the priciest toys and tastiest snacks. You must spend time with your child if their welfare is your priority. Unlike everything else that is material, time is irreplaceable.

Lead a Happier Life

Living a minimalistic lifestyle can benefit you in numerous ways. Having greater flexibility and making time to spend with loved ones are two of those. You will undoubtedly be satisfied if you use minimalist practices to assist yourself in paying off debt. Another method is to get rid of the things that bring you down.

Observing your mementos can cause intense feelings. Nevertheless, those feelings aren't always favorable. You can miss the moment if the souvenir is meant to bring back joyful memories. Having items that remind you of your difficulties and eventual accomplishments will help you appreciate the latter. However, you have a part of you that is a little depressed about your struggles.

Digital tokens of remembering are encouraged by minimalism as an alternative to physical memories. In this manner, the memories they arouse and the attachment to those objects won't be overly intense. More significantly, since you won't be scrolling through pictures as often, you'll have more control over when you need to recollect the happy and bad occasions. Should such keepsakes be hung on the wall, all it would take is a chance glance in their direction to bring back memories. You will be more likely to live in the moment if you don't have those constant reminders.

It is important to stay present-focused and not worry too much about the future. Besides, you only really have control over today. Start using that control by clearing out stuff, as the next chapter suggests.

Section Four

To live a fuller life, one must overcome addiction to convenience.

The worship of comfort and convenience is among the most harmful myths we can accept. We don't have the right to a convenient and comfortable life. We have a right to a second opportunity. We frequently travel to receive the shot, but we are undoubtedly not entitled to the outcome.

Unfortunately, far too many people think that way. It pulls them down and holds them back. Ultimately, our addiction to convenience is the main cause of many of the issues plaguing our culture.

Issues with Weight

Public health organizations and research teams concur that Americans are becoming slower and fatter overall over time, based on numerous studies. According to other surveys, Americans appear to be becoming less happy over time. We are obsessed with convenience, so these are all connected. Our dedication is almost slavish. We always want more convenience.

What you do with the time you have is the issue. You take a seat in front of a screen or computer. Instead of moving about or doing any type of physical activity, you spend endless hours in front of a tablet. We use the time our time-saving technology has freed up to lead nearly effortless lifestyles. As a result, we're growing older and older, bigger and heavier, and more unpleasant.

It may seem paradoxical, but contemporary Western culture is a victim of its prosperity. Why, in your opinion, are antidepressant and anti-anxiety meds consistently included among the top 10 most prescribed pharmaceuticals in the US? They complement one another. The more unhappy people get, the more comfortable their lives get.

Ways to Release Yourself

I will assist you in kicking your addiction to convenience in this chapter. Will this be a simple task? Not at all. Will you enjoy yourself during this event? Naturally, no. Is it required? I'll wager on it.

What should you do as a priority first? Start by taking the difficult route. Try climbing one flight of stairs instead of using the lift. I just need one flight of steps, please. Try it; you won't die doing it.

This is quite simple. It will irritate you at first. That's something I can give you, but the more times you do something, the more natural it becomes. Even little annoyances like parking far away can encourage you to lead a more passively physically active lifestyle if you find it difficult to get out of bed in the morning and go for a few laps around your block.

You are raising your daily activity level as long as you merely include it in your routine without giving it any thought. Although things get more awkward as a result, your mind adjusts. You may wait an hour or thirty minutes for pizza; the extra fifteen or forty-five minutes won't kill you. It turns out that you didn't need to park right next to the entrance. Who knew?

Take the difficult route. Gently crack the surface of your attachment to convenience. The good thing is that you may start scaling it up as soon as cracks begin to show. Your entire world did not collapse. You survived. You can put up with a little more inconvenience since you're still here.

Useful Advice: Take More Steps

You should strive to walk more often in addition to the distance you need to walk to get to your business or school. It's important to get up and move for around ten minutes every hour, even if your job as a freelancer is writing or dictating all day.

It won't end your life. Long periods spent sitting still have been linked to an increased risk of dying younger than expected. But walking more also helps to prepare your thoughts. By moving around more, you're not only jumping into short and simple things but also getting more exercise and paying attention to your surroundings. You also get a deeper appreciation for the things in your immediate environment.

Useful Advice: Take Your Time

Give yourself more time to wait. Never become agitated if you find yourself waiting in a queue. I am aware that many Americans lose their cool when they are required to wait more than thirty minutes.

Take out a pocketbook and begin reading to pass the time. At that time, you're doing two things. You're doing multiple tasks at once. Reading not only enhances your cognitive abilities but also requires you to stand in line to be at your appointment on time. Everything will work out. All you have to do is wait.

The Huge Gain

These things might not seem like much, but trust me when I say they pay off handsomely. To start with, you become more disciplined. I'm sure you don't need me to reiterate the significance of discipline.

Following through on important tasks when there are simpler, more convenient options is the essence of discipline. You work harder now to reap greater benefits later on. However, doing the easier things first will result in rewards of either inferior quality or level.

You become more patient by packing your day with more inconvenient activities. You have a lot more tolerance for other people's behavior. Additionally, you can work hard under challenging circumstances. It's human nature to choose the easiest route, let's face it.

It's much easier to leave rather than wait for a family member or significant other to get their act together. After all, who wants the trouble or inconvenience? You must stay in the relationship and persevere if you want it to succeed.

All of these have psychological benefits. Enjoy the procedure, watch life unfold, and discover more specifics. It's the little things that matter. Do you believe that if you can absorb as many of the "good things in life" as you can while traveling from point A to point B, you will score more points in the race that is life? Most likely not.

Consuming tobacco

The fact that smoking cigarettes is on the list of black holes shouldn't be shocking. On this list, smoking is perhaps the biggest problem due to the harm it causes and the huge amount of people it affects. Additionally, according to CDC estimates, smoking cigarettes causes over 480,000 deaths annually in the US.

For years, I smoked a lot. I was smoking about twenty-five cigarettes a day when I stopped. Before going to bed in the end, I would smoke my "last" cigarette, put the butt out, and then take out, light, and smoke another right away. It was then that I saw I had a major issue that would only worsen—I was chain-smoking two cigarettes before bed since one wasn't enough anymore. I gave up. As of the day I'm writing this, I have spared myself from smoking more than 53,000 cigarettes since I gave up. I did some maths and discovered that 53,000 cigarettes come to more than $20,000. That is the very least. Given the current state of cigarette costs, the true monetary sum is likely far larger.

Smoking is a money and health stealer, but it also takes away from your time. If you smoke one pack of cigarettes a day, which takes three minutes, you will be smoking for an hour each day. Smoking an hour a day adds up to FIFTY DAYS of smoking cigarettes annually. That's the amount of time you spend smoking directly, but what about indirectly? Snuffing out one's butt, emptying the ashtray, walking outdoors, and sitting by the window all require time. Stopping to buy cigarettes also takes time. In addition to using up mental resources, smoking causes you to constantly consider your next cigarette, particularly if it has been an hour or two since your last one.

What are the advantages of smoking? What does it return to you after all the money and effort you put into it? Does it truly make you think more clearly or work more quickly? Does it make you feel better when you're sad? Does smoking help people around you and your loved ones? The only thing you gain from smoking may be the ability to get rid of the withdrawal symptoms from your LAST cigarette. You lose everything when you smoke, and you never get it back. This is not a black hole; some might be fine in moderation.

booze

For some people, moderate alcohol use doesn't seem to be a problem; for others, however, it can develop into a horrible addiction. Alcohol has the power to destroy lives. While it may not be a black hole for everyone, alcohol has the potential to become one. You definitely won't get sucked in if you have one or two drinks every few weeks, but if you have to have a few after work every night and then a few more on the weekends, you might be staring into the abyss.

Alcoholism can have a major negative impact on one's physical and mental health. In essence, ethanol is a weak poison and the sense of intoxication we experience is caused by the poison seeping into our bodies. Long-term poisoning episodes can lead to cirrhosis of the liver and an elevated risk of certain malignancies, among other major health complications. It's risky even in the short term because drinking too much alcohol quickly can be lethal. When alcohol is given up abruptly, even quitting can be deadly.

A single evening spent at a pub with pals can potentially deplete a heavy drinker's whole weekly income. Drinks don't come cheap. Even a few drinks over an hour or two can cost you $50 or more. Although it doesn't become a black hole for everyone, alcohol has a lot of potential. Alcohol is a drug, even though it is commonly taken and lawful in most locations. As such, it is best used sparingly.

Medications

Although alcohol, caffeine, and nicotine are all regarded as drugs, I'll limit my discussion to street drugs and prescription drug misuse because I've already addressed the majority of them separately.

People yet use them. While Rachael Leigh Cook's iconic frying pan incident in the "YOUR BRAIN ON DRUGS" PSA may stick in people's memories, has it truly stopped anyone from developing a drug addiction?

Drugs are a frequent and deadly black hole that may draw you in so deeply that you end up spending all of your money, time, and attention chasing them. They have the power to wreck your life and steal you from your health and judgment. Some individuals have such severe addictions that they may rob cash and belongings from friends and relatives to purchase narcotics. To obtain narcotics, some people will engage in sexual acts, break into homes, or even rob others at gunpoint. Hardcore drug addiction and a minimalist lifestyle don't exactly go along. Hopefully, you have plenty of reasons not to become addicted to drugs, but add a minimalist lifestyle to your list of motivations.

www.ingramcontent.com/pod-product-compliance
Lightning Source LLC
Chambersburg PA
CBHW052142110526
44591CB00012B/1822